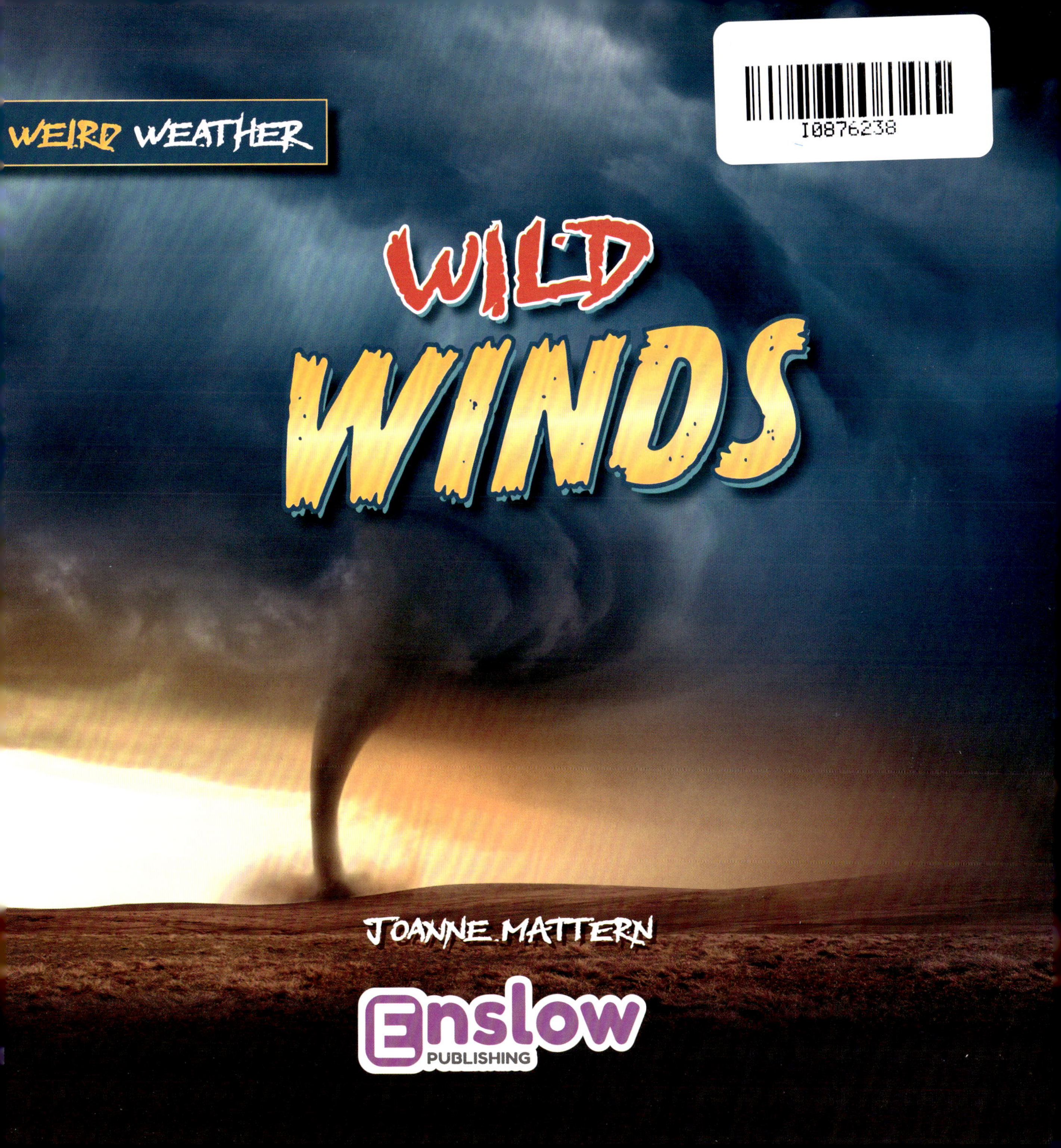

WEIRD WEATHER

WILD WINDS

JOANNE MATTERN

Enslow PUBLISHING

Please visit our website, www.enslow.com. For a free color catalog of all our high-quality books,
call toll free 1-800-398-2504 or fax 1-877-980-4454

Published in 2027 by
Enslow Publishing
2544 Clinton Street
Buffalo, NY 14224

Cataloging-in-Publication Data
Names: Mattern, Joanne, 1963-.
Title: Wild winds / Joanne Mattern.
Description: Buffalo, NY : Enslow Publishing, 2027. | Series: Weird weather | Includes glossary.
Identifiers: ISBN 9781978549845 (pbk.) | ISBN 9781978549852 (library bound) | ISBN 9781978549869 (ebook)
Subjects: LCSH: Winds--Juvenile literature. | Hurricanes--Juvenile literature. | Tornadoes--Juvenile literature. | Weather--Juvenile literature.
Classification: LCC QC931.4 M375 2027 | DDC 551.518--dc23

Photos Credits: Cover, p.1 ©2013 solarseven/Shutterstock.com; p.3 and throughout the book ©2020 Cherisha Kay Norman/Shutterstock.com; p.4, p.29 © 2023Vibe Images/Shutterstock.com; p.4 public domain/NOAA: Iron County Historical Society; p.5 public domain/NOAA: Indiana State Library Archives; p.6 public domain/NOAA: Jackson County Historical Society, p.6, p.7 ©2025 Chad Cowan/Shutterstock.com; p.8 ©2013 Scott Prokop/Shutterstock.com; p.9 ©2022 Chad Robertson Media/Shutterstock.com; p.10, p.11 ©2024 JP Midwest Storm Chaser/Shutterstock.com; p.12 ©2025 Stefan Klein/Shutterstock.com; p.13, p.28 ©2014 Minerva Studio/Shutterstock.com; p.14 © 2023 Stonery84/Shutterstock.com; p.15, p.28 ©2018 Candice Trimble/Shutterstock.com; p.16, p.17 ©2025 trandafirastoica/Shutterstock.com; p.18 ©2020 Eddie J. Rodriquez/Shutterstock.com; p.19, p.29 ©2024 Maximillian cabinet/Shutterstock.com; p.20 ©2022 muratart/Shutterstock.com; p.21 ©2024 Slim Segi/Shutterstock.com; p.22, p.23, p.29 ©2024 John D Sirlin/Shutterstock.com; p.24 ©2015 Everett Collection/Shutterstock.com; p.25, p.26 ©2015 Everett Collection/Shutterstock.com; p.26, p.27 ©2020 Stanley Dullea/Shutterstock.com

Printed in China

CPSIA compliance information: Batch #QSENS27: For further information, contact Enslow Publishing, New York, New York, at 1-800-398-2504.

TABLE OF CONTENTS

Words in the glossary appear in **bold** type the first time they are used in the text.

THREE HOURS OF TERROR

The people of Annapolis, Missouri, had no idea what hit them. At 1:15 p.m. on March 18, 1925, a "smoky fog" touched down. But this was not fog. It was a tornado. In seconds, 90 percent of the town was destroyed. And that was only the beginning.

TORNADO DESTRUCTION IN ANNAPOLIS, MISSOURI

PRINCETON CLARION-NEWS

TORNADO WRECKS SOUTH PRINCETON—TOLL OF DEAD 21

Over 200 Injured; 500 Homes Are Destroyed

Many Heart Aches Where Injured Lie

LITTLE GIRLS ORPHANED LIE SERIOUSLY HURT AT HOSPITAL—WRECK OF SOUTHERN SHOPS AND H. J. HEINZ PLANT COMPLETE

THE DEAD

Scenes of Horror As Families Are Separated and Injured Men, Women and Children are Carried to Hospitals—Southern Shops and H. J. Heinz Plant, Prides of Princeton, Demolished by Terrific Wind

SERIOUSLY INJURED

BALDWIN HEIGHTS SCHOOL IN PRINCETON, INDIANA, BEFORE AND AFTER THE TORNADO STRUCK.

The tornado crossed the Mississippi River into Illinois. It then moved into Indiana. For three and a half hours, the tornado stayed on the ground. Its destructive path across three states gave the storm its name: the Tri-State Tornado.

The Tri-State Tornado was the most damaging tornado in United States history. Scientists think wind speeds reached more than 300 miles (483 kilometers) per hour. The tornado killed 695 people and injured 2,000 others. The storm traveled 219 miles (352 kilometers). Those are records that still stand today.

Entire towns were destroyed. Powerful winds carried items hundreds of miles away. It ripped grass right out of the ground. All that damage was caused by the storm's wild winds.

TORNADO DESTRUCTION IN MURFYSBORO, ILLINOIS

SUPER STRENGTH

One man found a document that had been in a bank safe 125 miles (201 kilometers) away.

TWISTING AND TURNING

A tornado is the most **violent** storm on Earth. It begins as a funnel cloud. A funnel cloud is a **column** of air that spins and drops downward. When the funnel cloud touches the ground, it becomes a tornado.

A tornado usually lasts for less than 15 minutes. But in that short time, these storms can cause massive destruction.

Tornado winds can be strange. A storm might destroy houses on one side of the street but not the other. It might knock down one tree but leave the one next to it still standing. No one can predict what a tornado will do!

STORMY WEATHER

Tornadoes usually form during a thunderstorm. About 1,200 tornadoes strike the U.S. every year.

Scientists measure tornadoes using the Enhanced Fujita Scale. This scale assigns a number to a tornado. That number is based on wind speed and **damage**. An EF0 tornado is not very strong. The worst tornadoes measure EF5. An EF5 tornado has winds of more than 200 miles (322 kilometers) per hour.

Before **meteorologists** could measure tornadoes, they could only guess how strong the wind was. They made guesses based on how much damage a tornado did.

Enhanced Fujita Scale

EF Rating	Speed of Wind **Gusts**
0	65–85 miles per hour
1	86–110 miles per hour
2	111–135 miles per hour
3	136–165 miles per hour
4	166–200 miles per hour
5	Over 200 miles per hour

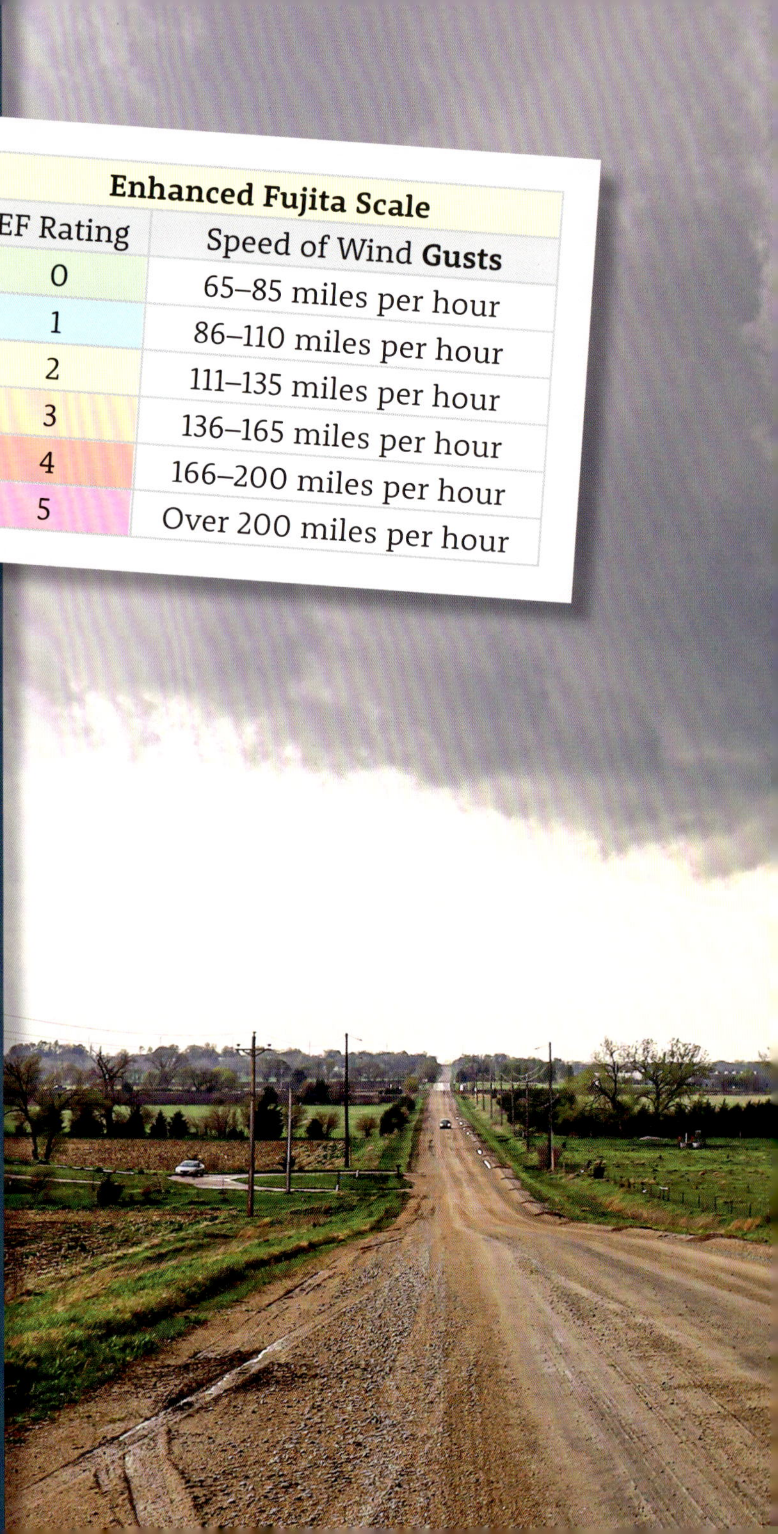

TORNADOES LIVE HERE

So many tornadoes happen in the central United States that the area is called Tornado Alley.

WET AND WILD

It’s usually easy to see a tornado over land. It is made up of dirt and debris. It is big and dark.

But sometimes water can be lifted up and spun around. This is called a waterspout. Waterspouts can be dangerous. They can overturn ships.

There are two kinds of waterspouts. Tornadic waterspouts form when tornadoes from land move over water. Fair weather waterspouts form over water. Swirling winds stir up the surface of the water and lift it into the sky.

WHERE ARE THE WATERSPOUTS?

More waterspouts form in the Florida Keys than anywhere else on Earth.

BURSTING OUT!

Sometimes thunderstorms cause downbursts. A downburst is a powerful area of cold air that moves down. This movement creates strong gusts of wind. Small bursts are called microbursts. Big ones are called macrobursts. These bursts can be strong enough to knock down trees and power lines.

Wind is not the only danger from a microburst. If the air is **humid**, some microbursts can produce heavy rainfall. A dry microburst has no rain.

WOW, IT'S WINDY!

A microburst can produce winds up to 168 miles (270 kilometers) per hour.

Microbursts can be a problem for airplanes. A microburst's winds can cause a pilot to lose control of the plane. This is most likely to happen during landings.

Microbursts also cause wind shear. During wind shear, the winds change direction or speed very quickly. This can make an airplane very difficult to fly.

In 1985, a flight crashed at a Texas airport because of a microburst. More than 130 people were killed. Today, pilots are trained on how to deal with microbursts. Airports also have better ways to detect them.

WINDSTORM AHEAD!

Derechos are another powerful windstorm. Many people confuse derechos with tornadoes. Both storms include powerful winds and come with thunderstorms. But they are not the same. Tornadoes spin around. They can move in unexpected ways. Derechos move straight ahead. They can cover a lot of ground.

A derecho has winds of at least 58 miles (93 kilometers) per hour. They can be more than 400 miles (644 kilometers) long and 60 miles (96.5 kilometers) across. That's a lot of wind!

THE RIGHT KIND OF STORM

These storms got their name from the Spanish word derecho. *Derecho means "right" or "straight ahead."*

LET'S GET SANDY

Some winds bring rain. Others bring ... sand? That's right! When wind and sand get together, things can get wild! Sandstorms happen when strong winds pick up sand and dust from the ground. The winds push the sand into giant clouds.

Most sandstorms occur near deserts and other dry areas. But sandstorms can affect areas far from where they start. Winds carry dust and dirt over big cities. This makes the air hard to breathe. Millions of people can be affected by sandstorms.

Sandstorms cause damage in other ways too. They can bury roads and buildings. They can make it hard to see. Many car crashes happen in sandstorms because drivers can't see the road.

A haboob is a kind of sandstorm. It is caused by a thunderstorm. Haboobs form when strong winds in a storm blow down to the ground. These winds pick up dirt and sand. The cold air in front of a thunderstorm pushes the dirt forward.

Haboobs can grow to a giant size. They can travel as far as 100 miles (161 kilometers).

ON THE MAP

Haboobs are common in the southwestern United States.

THE DUST BOWL

The wind can have a huge impact on our lives. Between 1930 and 1936, sandstorms struck the central United States. The area became so dry that it was called the Dust Bowl.

There were two big reasons for the Dust Bowl. One was a **drought**. Very little rain fell. The other problem was that people had **plowed** much of the grass to farm new land. There were no plant roots to hold on to the soil. When the winds came, the soil blew away. Millions of people left their homes to escape the dust and all the damage it caused.

HARD TO BREATHE

Some people died of "dust pneumonia" when their lungs became full of dust.

The worst day of the Dust Bowl became known as Black Sunday. On that day, a huge black cloud of dust raced across the land. It was pushed by 100-mile (161-kilometer) per hour winds. The sky was as dark as night. The dust was so thick, people could not see their hands in front of their faces. It was hard to breathe.

Black Sunday showed people that weather can be wild and dangerous. Today, better weather forecasting helps us learn about wild winds before they happen. But you never know when the next crazy windstorm might strike!

WHAT AM I?

Can you guess what type of wild wind is shown in each photo? Look closely at these images and use the clues to help you figure it out. Then, check your answers below. How many did you get right?

1

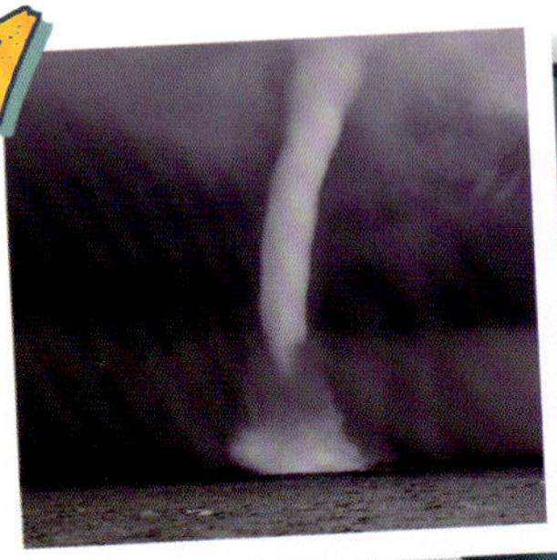

Like water going down the drain, I spin around and around where wind meets the wet stuff. What am I?

2

You'll feel my crazy winds when I zoom down from the clouds! What am I?

3

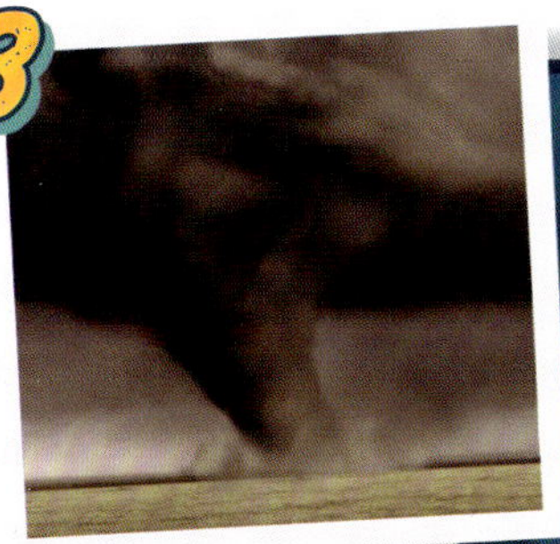

I twist and weave and zig and zag. You never know what my powerful winds will destroy! What am I?

4

I make the sky black and blow dirt in your face. You'd best get inside if you see my dark cloud. What am I?

5

Some people think I'm like a tornado, but I prefer straight lines to zigzags. What am I?

1. water spout; 2. downburst; 3. tornado; 4. haboob; 5. derecho

GLOSSARY

column (KAH-luhm): a tall tube shape

damage (DAM-ij): when something is broken or destroyed

drought (DROUT): a long period with little or no rainfall

gusts (GUHSTS): sudden bursts of wind

humid (HYOO-mid): full of moisture and usually very warm in a way that is uncomfortable

meteorologists (mee-tee-uh-RAH-luh-jists): scientists who study the weather

plowed (PLOUD): broke up soil using a piece of farm equipment

violent (VY-uh-lent): strong and destructive

FACT CHECK

1. The wind in a tornado ___________.
   a. spins around b. blows straight down c. blows in a straight line
2. When wind changes direction very suddenly, it is called ___________.
   a. a thunderstorm b. wind shear c. a microburst
3. The Dust Bowl happened when the wind picked up ___________.
   a. grass b. plants c. soil

Answers: 1. a, 2. b, 3. c

FURTHER READING

Kenney, Karen Latchana. *The Dust Bowl.* Bearport Publishing, 2024.

Locher, Wes. *Where is Tornado Alley?* Penguin Random House, 2025.

Mattern, Joanne. *The Worst Tornadoes on Record.* Mitchell Lane Publishers, 2025.

ON THE INTERNET

Microburst

www.britannica.com/science/microburst

This Britannica article explains how microbursts form and the danger they can cause.

Tornadoes

https://kids.nationalgeographic.com/science/article/tornado

This National Geographic Kids article includes lots of interesting facts and dramatic photos of tornadoes.

Publisher's note to educators and parents: Our editors have carefully reviewed these websites to ensure that they are suitable for students. Many websites change frequently, however, and we cannot guarantee that a site's future contents will continue to meet our high standards of quality and educational value. Be advised that students should be closely supervised whenever they access the internet.

INDEX

ABOUT THE AUTHOR

Joanne Mattern is the author of many books for children on a variety of subjects, including science, history, and biography. She loves writing about and experiencing weird weather events! Joanne loves to learn about people, places, and events and bring historical figures to life for today's readers. She lives in New York State with her family.